BIRD PORTRAITURE

"HOW TO DO IT" SERIES

Others in preparation.

BIRD
PORTRAITURE

By C. F. Tunnicliffe

"HOW TO DO IT"
SERIES NO. 35

THE STUDIO :
LONDON & NEW YORK

First published   January, 1945
Second impression November, 1946

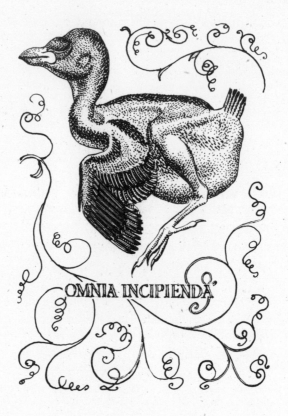

OMNIA INCIPIENDA

Reg. U.S.
STUDIO
Pat. Off.

Printed in England by Balding & Mansell Ltd., Park Works,
Wisbech, Cambridgeshire, and Published in London by The
Studio Ltd., 66 Chandos Place, W.C.2, and in New York by
The Studio Publications Inc., 381 Fourth Avenue.

CONTENTS

667761

COLOUR PLATES

LIST OF ILLUSTRATIONS IN MONOCHROME

Grebe in Spring

INTRODUCTION

FROM the time when man first scratched images on bone and rock, artists have, in a multitude of different ways, depicted birds, whose power to leave the earth at will and to speed through the air has ever aroused the wonder and envy of humans, and has also been responsible for many legends and superstitions : for, however familiar we are with birds, they never seem to lose their strangeness. They are a form of life quite unique—very different from earth-bound man and animals, yet having points of similarity with them which only serve to accentuate this difference. In the process of evolution they have become perfectly adapted to that mode of life which is necessary for their survival, and this adaptation has brought in its train much beauty, offering endless variety of subject matter for the artist.

The quality of this beauty is difficult to define, but, to me, it has a great affinity with that of flowers. It is of the bird, and does not depend on any special condition, excepting that of light, for its revelation. It is true that certain environments enhance it, but if it were possible to see a bird apart from everything else it would still be a beautiful creature. So much for the intrinsic beauty of our subject for portraiture. It is with the creation of a very different kind of beauty that this book will try to deal,—that of line and form and colour on paper or canvas ; a work of art in fact which, we hope, will have its own particular claim to be beautiful, not because it has slavishly imitated the form and colour of the bird, but because it has used the bird and controlled it to create a new beauty.

Then what a prodigious amount of arduous and enjoyable work lies before you! There will be great days out of doors, studying from life, when so much is happening that one is at a loss to know where to start or what to draw ; other days of landscape drawing ; still others for the noting of bird habitats, plumage studies, and, if you are wise, a certain amount of work among the specimens in museums, for it is good to draw and paint with confidence and knowledge. Without scientific understanding of your subjects you will inevitably encounter much that will puzzle you : with it you will be able to comprehend and appreciate more fully the wild bird, since it is to the living creature that you will always return if your work is to have vitality and freshness. And what better company could you desire than that of these lively, vivacious creatures which combine beauty and grace in such inexhaustible variety ?

Tawny Owl

Bantam Cock

MAKING A BEGINNING

It would be foolish to attempt to lay down any hard and fast rules for the practice of bird-painting, for, of course, there are none. It will, therefore, be more to the point if I tell you of my own experiences and conclusions, from which you can extract whatever you may find helpful, and discard the rest. I do not remember the first birds I drew, but it is probable that they were the hens and ducks of the farm ; and these I would recommend to you, for they are tame, and much more accessible than wild birds. Later, and as a further step towards the study of the wild bird, you may be able to visit a Zoo and exercise your growing facility on the birds there, but you will find the homely farm-yard fowl good subjects for first practice.

If you get an opportunity to handle them, do not neglect it, because you will then be able to observe the various groups of feathers, and to feel the bony construction of wings and legs, all of which will be a great help to you in understanding the anatomy, not only of farmyard fowl, but of other birds also ; for, although anatomy differs considerably in the various species, the fundamental construction of the skeleton is similar in most birds, as also is the grouping of the feathers, though this, too, is subject to great variation. So it would be wisdom to familiarise yourself with the skeleton of a bird first and with the arrangement of the feathers afterwards. For the latter, the study of stuffed birds is helpful, *but only for the feather details*. Do not use the stuffed bird as a substitute for the living creature. Rarely does one find a mounted specimen that in any way reproduces the form of the wild bird ; for, in the former, all muscular tension is lost, and no amount of craftsmanship on the part of the taxidermist can breathe life into its poor, dried skin. However, the art of taxidermy is improving, and presently we may see reasonably good representations of the live bird.

If you examine the drawing of the bird's skeleton you will notice certain points of similarity to the human skeleton. The bird has fore-limbs which have become the wing bones ; it has leg bones consisting of femur, tibia and tarsus ; but here a big difference occurs, for the bird's femur is not free, as is that of man, but is connected by tissues to the side of the bird. The joint which we are in the habit of calling the leg-joint in a bird really corresponds to the human ankle, and all the bony portion below that joint, the tarsus, is the true foot. So it will be seen that most birds walk on their toes, although there are a few which use the whole of the true foot as support. But, for the purpose of this book, the term " leg " will be used to denote the forms immediately above and below the leg-joint and the term " foot " to indicate that portion which is in contact with the ground when the bird is standing.

Now let us look at the drawings of the feather anatomy of three very different birds. These are drawn to demonstrate the way the feathers are split up into definite groups over the body of the bird, and also to show the great variation in shape and mass of the groups. But, in spite of these variations, it will be seen that the same groups are present in each bird. For the bird student, a knowledge of these feather formations is absolutely essential, as birds can move any one of these groups independently of the rest, a fact you will soon prove for yourself if you watch them when they preen, display emotion, or react to the state of the weather. So, for your further pleasure, make yourself familiar with these anatomical details.

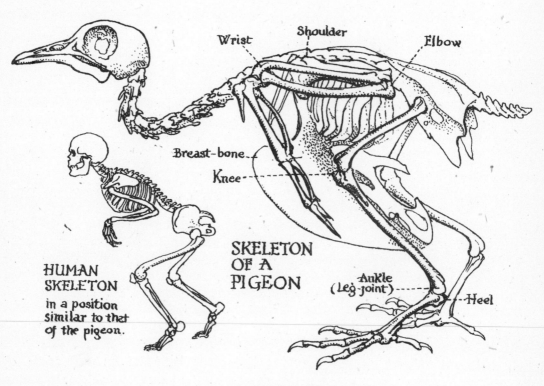

Skeleton of a Bird

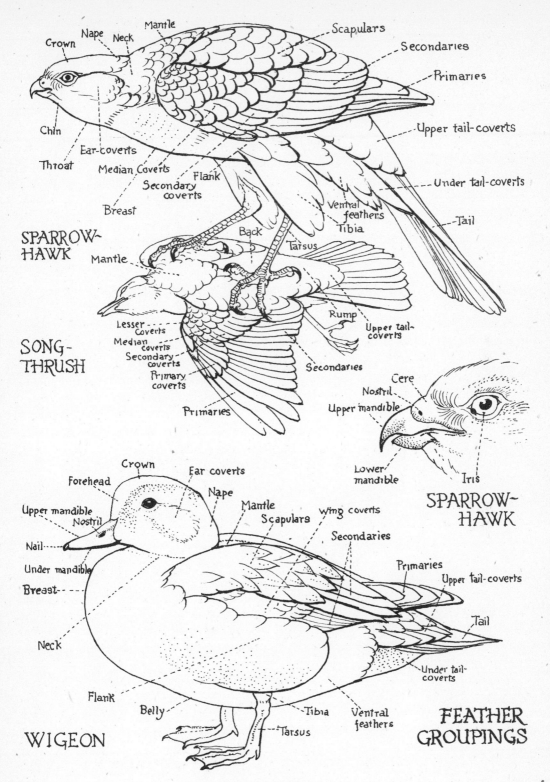

Crown
Nape
Neck
Mantle
Scapulars
Secondaries
Primaries
Chin
Ear-coverts
Throat
Median Coverts
Secondary coverts
Breast
Flank
Back
Tarsus
Ventral feathers
Tibia
Upper tail-coverts
Under tail-coverts
Tail

SPARROW-HAWK

Mantle

SONG-THRUSH

Lesser Coverts
Median coverts
Secondary coverts
Primary coverts
Primaries
Secondaries
Rump
Upper tail-coverts

Cere
Nostril
Upper mandible
Lower mandible
Iris

SPARROW-HAWK

Crown
Forehead
Ear coverts
Nape
Upper mandible
Nostril
Mantle
Scapulars
Wing coverts
Secondaries
Nail
Under mandible
Breast
Primaries
Upper tail-coverts
Tail
Neck
Under tail-coverts
Flank
Belly
Tibia
Tarsus
Ventral feathers

WIGEON

FEATHER GROUPINGS

Feather Groupings

II

Sketches of Poultry

A Farmyard Goose

DRAWING FROM LIFE

Presently, after you have practised drawing hens, and perhaps the farm ducks and geese, you will realise that each type of bird has its own character, its own "architecture," so to speak. There is a vast difference in the shape of the various breeds, the heaviness of the Rhode Island Reds contrasting, for example, with the sprightliness of the White Leghorns. Later you will see also that each individual bird has a character peculiar to itself, one bird being only superficially like its neighbour. Now contrast the shape of the hens with that of the geese, and of the geese with that of the ducks. How very different and individual they all are ! And, if you keep a budgerigar, an examination of its shape and character will provide yet another great contrast of bird form.

Whilst trying to draw and master the shape of these tame birds, you will no doubt have gazed longingly on the wild birds as they flashed past or soared above, or perched for a few all-too-short seconds on a branch near by, and you will have wondered how a study of these restless and wary creatures was to be made. We must bear in mind that, as a rule, the close presence of humans is intolerable to a wild bird, and that, after a short period of alert watchfulness, it usually leaves the vicinity. It is desirable, therefore, to conceal oneself, or to devise some means of studying the bird at a distance, so that it is not aware of a human presence and thus goes about its business in a natural manner. A good pair of field glasses is essential for this long distance work.

Of course, there are occasions when birds are tolerant of human presence and remain in close view for some length of time, but these must be counted as fortunate moments, and should be used to full advantage when they do occur. As a rule, unless the bird is asleep, there is often quite lively movement, and one cannot draw a pose when it is not retained by the model for more than a few seconds. How then can we make drawings of the quick-moving bird? I know of only one way, and that is to watch, and watch, and watch again. Do not attempt to draw while you have the bird in view, but try to get accurate impressions photographed on your mind, so that when the bird finally disappears you can get to work on your sketch book and set down these impressions at once. In using this method you will find your previous study of anatomy most useful, for, by its aid, you will have understood and fixed in your mind many of the bird's movements.

Young Rook.   Study from life of an Injured Bird

Reed Warbler Feeding Young.   Drawn immediately after studying the birds for over an hour

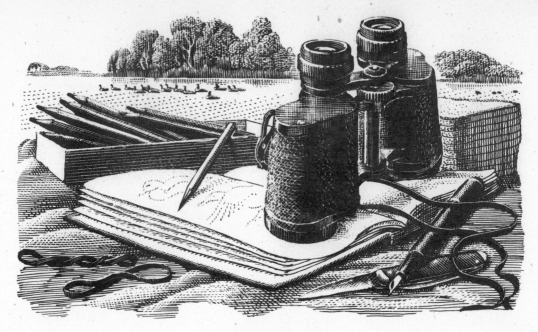

Equipment for Field Work

EQUIPMENT FOR FIELD WORK

Great care should be taken in choosing equipment for your " field work "—the term used by ornithologists for the study of the wild bird in its natural habitat. The maximum amount of efficiency and comfort should be aimed at, for the study of wild birds is arduous enough, without the added difficulty of unsatisfactory materials and conditions.

I have found that a sketch book measuring about 9ins. by 6ins. is large enough to take several sketches on a page, and small enough to slip into the pocket of a mackintosh : and do not forget a couple of elastic bands to keep the leaves of the book in position if there is much wind while you are at work. I use a H.B. pencil for quick notes, and I have in reserve a fountain pen filled with dark brown or black ink in case I want to draw a darker line on top of my pencil notes. For quick colour notes I carry a collection of coloured pencils and find these very satisfactory, because the results are always dry and in no danger of smudging. Moreover, one can turn the page and draw on the next without delay, which would not be possible if paint were used. Should I feel that the addition of white would be a help in making my sketch impression more correct in tone, I wait until I get home, and then use a white body-colour for that purpose. A sharp penknife is also indispensable.

When drawing birds out of doors you will often be forced to adopt a variety of attitudes in which to work,—standing, sitting, kneeling, or lying,—and you will probably find that by far the most efficient position in which to draw is to lie full length on your stomach, with sketch book resting on the ground, field glasses held in one hand, and pencil in the other. So I suggest that another very useful item of equipment would be an old mackintosh which is still waterproof. This you could often use as a ground sheet, for the pursuit of birds will, at times, lead you into all sorts of wet, sodden places, such as marshes, river-sides, and seaweed-covered rocks ; and some places will be too wet even for a ground sheet.

Now, about the all-important question of field glasses. Be sure to obtain a good pair, for they are your second pair of eyes, and the more efficient they are the more pleasure you will have in your work. Binoculars of eight magnifications are powerful enough, as it is difficult to hold steady an instrument of greater power. Your glasses should have as wide a field of view as possible, for you must remember that you will be studying birds in flight as well as those on the ground or on the water, and the wider the field of view the easier it will be to pick up a flying bird. They should be of the centre-screw focussing type. When not in use they should always be kept in their leather case : never put them in your pocket.

Then, with a few sandwiches stowed in a knapsack,—close concentration in the fresh air is hungry work—you are ready for whatever bird may turn up.

Too Wet for a Ground Sheet

A FIELD DAY

In this little book there is not sufficient space to give you even the scantiest description of all the birds it is possible to meet in a land so favoured by birds as ours. There is no doubt that our country is exceptionally favoured, for the British Isles lies directly in the path of many migratory birds, and these, added to those birds which are resident with us all the year round, make an imposing list.

So perhaps, for the purpose of noting a few, it might be as well if we walked abroad on some fine October morning, when the brown leaves are beginning to pile up by the hedges, and many of the birds, which have spent their summer elsewhere, are coming to grace the Cheshire landscape for a time. . . . . ! "Why Cheshire ?" you ask. Only because it is the countryside in which I have done most of my bird study . . . . . . A short bus journey takes us well out of sight of the town, and we leave the vehicle at the cross roads and turn into a narrow lane which is canopied with the branches of tall beeches. The road climbs under the branches until, at its top, there is a sudden clear view of the Cheshire Plain to the west, and of the East Cheshire hills to the east ; here also is a wide prospect of rich ploughland and farms, and many birds are about. First to attract our attention is a mixed flock of Lapwings and Starlings which sweeps across our lane as it passes from one ploughed field to another. What a great contrast there

Lapwing Flock

Lapwing, Rook, Starlings and Wood-pigeons

is in the flight and appearance of the two species ! The Starlings pour over the road with a rushing sound, in close formation of arrow-head shapes, while the Lapwings flap across in a much more leisurely fashion, their round-ended wings beating much slower than those of the Starlings. The first birds to land are the Starlings, and so quickly do they alight that the manner of their landing is difficult to follow ; but watch the Lapwings ! Down they plane, gliding low over the ground, and then, braking with wings and tails, touch ground, and for a second or two stand with wings full open, before bringing them into their sides—a most beautiful manoeuvre to watch, for the pattern of the open-winged bird is exquisite and well worth noting. The Lapwings are examined closely through the glasses, and we observe that their plumage shows many variations. A number of birds are browner than the rest, and have shorter crests ; these are the young birds which were hatched in the spring.

Higher up the field are some Rooks and, with them, a flock of Wood-pigeons. Watch the Rooks walk. Rather amusing with their flank feathers drooping like great trousers about their legs ! Neither Rooks nor Wood-pigeons like my scouting with the glasses, and those nearest take flight. All the Wood-pigeons now become alarmed and take refuge in the wood near by, spreading their tails and showing white wing patches as they sweep up into the branches of the oaks and beeches. Our road skirts this wood and, as we draw near, the pigeons take flight again and rise from the trees with a great clatter. When they have all gone all is quiet by the wood, and the only sound to be

Wood-pigeon rising

Startled Pheasant

heard is the rustle made by our feet as we walk through the crisp, dry leaves by the roadside. Suddenly, a cock Pheasant, which had crouched unseen in the dead leaves, rattles up with a great to-do, tail spread and neck outstretched, almost from under our feet. He wheels and twists between the tree trunks, and finally pitches behind a bank of bracken of the same tawny gold and russet colour as himself. In his noisy progress he disturbs a Jay, which is visible for a second as it flies deeper into the thicket, betrayed only by a flash of blue on the wings, a white rump, and the usual harsh and derisive call.

Soon the wood is left behind, and again fields stretch on either side of the road. In a tall ash tree some distance in front is a company of birds which, as we approach, leaves the branches and alights on the rough pasture to the right. Some are about the size of a Song Thrush, the others slightly larger. They are a company of Redwings and Fieldfares, both of the Thrush family, but resident with us during the winter and spring only : their home is in Scandinavia. Peep over the hedge and watch them for a

Fieldfare and Golden Plover

while. Note the upstanding carriage of the Fieldfares and the distinctive way they carry their wings —usually below the level of the tail. Compare their attitude with that of the more homely Redwings, which are more like our own Song Thrush in build. Hello ! what are those birds, just beyond the Fieldfares, resembling the dead grass tussocks so closely that we had not noticed them ? Glasses to work again ! Golden Plover they prove to be : lovely, delicate-looking birds with pale breasts, and gold-and-black-spangled backs. They stand now as upright as the Fieldfares, and appear about the same size. In spite of their looks they are not really delicate, for they perform prodigies of long distance flying with those beautiful, sharply pointed wings. They are real " globe-trotters."

But we must hurry on, or we shall never reach our destination to-day. Soon our winding lane begins to descend, cutting deep between high banks and hedges from which flocks of Chaffinches rise at intervals. These are mostly cock birds, and their rosy breasts and flashing white-marked wings look lovely among the green-gold of the autumn hawthorns.

Cock Chaffinch

From over the hedge comes the sound of a voice, " Bonny, git on ! Prince ! cum up !" Lower down the hill, hedge and bank are not so high, and in the sloping field on our right is a fine sight : a team of dappled-grey horses, guided effortlessly (or so it seems) by the teamsman, is ploughing the stubble and turning up the chocolate-brown earth in long, gleaming furrows. The team is closely followed by a cloud of Gulls which swoop to the new-turned earth, peck at something in the furrow, then take wing again, only to make another pounce. There must be about fifty Gulls following that plough, and what a noisy crowd they are ! Let us put the glasses on them. We soon see that all are Black-headed Gulls, that species of gull which in recent years has invaded the inland areas in greater and greater numbers.

The name " Black-headed " does not seem to fit them to-day, for there is not a black head amongst them : they are in winter plumage, and all that remains of the black (or more correctly dark sepia) head of the breeding plumage is a spot behind the eye and a dusky mark running over the crown above the ear-spot. If you look closely, you will also see that some of the Gulls have brown feathers on the wings and a dark sepia bar across the end of the tail. These are the distinguishing marks of a young bird. If you could see the colour of their beaks and legs, you would notice that they

Black-headed Gulls following the Plough

The Edge of the Mere

also differ from those of the mature birds. The beak and legs of the adult are a beautiful red, while the beak of the young bird is pale straw-coloured with a dark tip, and its legs a dull yellow. (See page 43).

How elegant is their flight! Note how they almost hover as they inspect the furrows. Above the lower part of the field there is some real hovering going on. Watch that dark, flickering spot for a time. There, it has slipped out of its hovering position, but after a short, banking turn has come round, head to wind, to hover again : our friend the Kestrel, of course, doing a useful job of work among the mice and voles. Now he is dropping, as if let down on a string, ... another hesitating hover . . . . . and then a final drop to ground. He's out of sight behind a hedge and, as he is staying down, his hunting has probably been successful.

At the bottom of the hill the lane runs level for a mile, at the end of which we catch, through the tree trunks of a long wood, glimpses of steel-grey water. Moorhens dash across the road in front of us, white under-tail coverts flashing as they run. Did you notice their long green toes, neat compact bodies, and sealing-wax-red bills ? At the end of the trees our destination is in full view, a fine stretch of water—a typical Cheshire mere. We linger first by a bed of reeds whose plumy tops curve and sway in the slight breeze. As we approach Coot scuttle from the reed-bed and make for the open water. We seem to have chosen a good day—with not too much breeze, and therefore very little ripple. The mere is dotted, here and there, with birds either singly or in companies, so let us examine the nearest to us first.

Less than thirty yards away, among the decaying leaves of the white water-lilies, sleeps a Great Crested Grebe. Note how this bird rests. It does not tuck its bill beneath the scapular feathers, as is the habit of many birds, but, instead, lays its neck back and rests the bill, which is pointing forward, on its breast to one side of the neck. This bird is worthy of observation for another reason ; it is in a very interesting state of plumage, for it is moulting from summer to winter dress. You will see that it has a little fringe of dusky feathers behind the eye; this fringe is all that is left of the resplendent

Resting Grebe

chestnut and black head-adornment of the breeding plumage. (See page 39). Presently it will moult nearly all of the fringe. Its flanks, too, are taking on the greyish plumage of winter. Another peculiarity of this very distinctive bird is that it has no tail, but is satisfied with a little tuft of down where the tail ought to be. A bird to draw ; so out with the sketch book, and to work before it rouses.

You have probably been casting interested glances at that flock of ducks resting some sixty or seventy yards out on the mere. They are Tufted Duck, a diving species of a very lively disposition, and get their name from the crest which curves gracefully down the back of their head and neck. The usual plumage of the drakes is black and white, but you will see that the white flanks of the drakes are now marked by smudges of dusky brown, denoting that they are still in what is described by ornithologists as " eclipse plumage." This "eclipse" is an intermediate plumage (adopted by most ducks about mid-summer), between the breeding and winter plumages. Some species of duck retain traces of their " eclipse " plumage much longer than others. Glance, for instance, at those Mallard resting on the half-submerged logs under the trees of the far shore. See how resplendent are the drakes with their metallic green-blue heads, bronze chests, silvery-grey flanks, and black curly tail feathers of their winter dress. Yet, in June and July, they were very different birds, almost as sober in plumage as their brown wives. Look again at that party of ten Shoveller ducks feeding among the

Tufted-Duck

Mallard (above) and Shovellers

persicaria ; there are four drakes in that party, yet not one of them is in full winter plumage, which, at its best, is even more colourful than that of the Mallard. All have many dark crescentic markings—remains of " eclipse " plumage—on what will become an almost pure white chest. So you see, this " eclipse " plumage is a phase which cannot be ignored. Tufted Duck, Mallard and Shoveller : how different they are in shape, yet all are ducks ; the first being dumpy and fat, the second having the familiar and orthodox duck shape, and the third possessing an amazing bill, which gives it its name. Try to draw the ducks while they are fairly quiet, and make a special effort to get the characteristic lines and poses of each species.

When you have finished your sketches, cast your eye aloft to that stump-like shape on the very top of the pine tree by the waterside. The glasses will reveal it to be a Heron at rest, with head and neck sunk between the shoulders, and with bill projecting from the top of the shoulders. He seems to be rousing ; ah ! now he is beginning to preen. Watch this carefully, for a Heron takes up some very fine attitudes when preening. Now he is wing-stretching ; what a fine shape he makes as he extends first one wing, then the other ! You will notice also that he stretches a leg at the same time and on the same side as the stretching wing. Soon, I expect, he will be off ; yes, there he goes : see how he holds his neck in an S bend during the first powerful strokes of his wings ; then, as he gets under way, tucks his neck back so that only the bill projects beyond his breast. Now he is well into his " stride," arched wings beating slowly and deliberately. However, he is not allowed to proceed far before some Rooks and Jackdaws appear as if from nowhere, and begin to harass the long-suffering Heron. There stoops a Rook, then a Jackdaw and now another Jackdaw. The Heron has to side-slip to avoid the rushes of his tormentors. Note the differences in the speed of the wing-beats of these three birds. The Heron has the slowest beats, the Rook's being considerably quicker, and the Jackdaw's quickest of all. Watch them well and try to memorise their flying shapes. One minute is all you will get for your study for the Heron is making straight for the tall trees of Boathouse Wood. Now he has pitched on top of another pine, and Rooks and Jackdaws leave him in peace. It is a curious fact that almost any bird will mob a flying heron : why, it is difficult to say ; for he is apparently harmless to other birds. Did you hear that high-pitched call from the alders away on the right ? That was made by a Kingfisher. Keep quiet, he may pass in our direction. Here he comes. . . . . . and there he goes, a line of electric blue, wings beating so rapidly that their detail could not be seen by the human eye. Not much time for study ! But someday, if you are standing very still by the waterside, you will have the luck to see a Kingfisher perch close to you, and possibly he will plunge for a fish—an exquisite experience you will never forget.

I wonder if you have been listening, this last half-minute, to a wild, yelping sound coming from away in the distance ; a two-note call in which the second note is higher than the first. It is coming steadily closer, and soon we may be treated to a grand sight. Fix your eyes on the sky just above the clump of tall beeches at the far end of the mere. There, do you see that line of birds just appearing ? What fine, strong wing-action they have ! Twenty-five Canada Geese in perfect formation, or so it would prove to be if we were below them, instead of directly in front, for then we should see that they were flying in V formation. Their wings are held in rigid curves as they come down to the water in a long glide. Watch their alighting, for it is a beautiful action. Nearer and nearer to the surface they sweep. Now they drop their feet, and soon, with wings and tails fully extended, they touch water, each bird ploughing the surface and sending a curve of spray from either flank as it comes to rest. A thrilling sight, I think you will agree.

Heron

After a clamorous burst of calling they settle down to cruise leisurely about the mere, then gradually approach the shallow bank where they often graze. Here you have a chance to compare goose shapes, for swimming by the bank are three tame Chinese Geese from the Vicarage. Note the difference in pose, and compare the racy lines of the Canadas with the "chunky" shapes of the Chinese. Observe also the difference in the way the species carry their tails ; those of the Chinese Geese, you see, point upwards, whilst the Canadas carry theirs low. Both species of geese now walk up the bank, and soon commence to graze, though you will notice that they do not mix, for the Canadas " keep themselves to themselves." I suggest that you sketch away at the geese for all you are worth, for they make fine pictures, and someday your drawings from life will prove most useful. The Canadas appear to be a little uneasy. Their necks are up, and they are muttering among themselves in low, subdued notes. The cause of their uneasiness is now seen, as across the field strides the head-keeper of the big estate, and at his heel are a retriever and a Springer spaniel. The Canadas sidle to the waterside, stride down the low bank, and walk in until they are afloat. I hope you noted the graceful curve of their necks as they walked down the bank : each bird holds its neck

Canadas planing down

Chinese Geese alarmed, and Canadas going to the Water

in the same position while taking the slope. From the water they watch the man and dogs disappear, and then return to their grazing on the bank.

The behaviour of the Chinese Geese towards the man and dogs was very different. These geese set up a great clamour and approached the intruders with necks and heads pointing skywards. As the man and dogs came closer the geese dropped their necks almost to the ground in a peculiar concave curve, and hissed fiercely at the dogs ; then, as the cause of their annoyance still came on, they turned aside, necks still extended, and followed the dogs, keeping some yards away from them until the birds decided that the intruders had departed.

Well ! I think you will most likely have had enough of birds for one day and, moreover, the wind is rising and conditions for bird watching and drawing are not so favourable as they were when we arrived. So take a final look at the flock of Tufted Duck now being rocked by the little waves running before the wind : and at the noisy crowd of Rooks and Jackdaws spiralling high up above the wood called Parson's Rough. They seem to be taking keen pleasure in their powers of flight and their ability to use the boisterous air above the tree-tops, for they scarcely move their wings in this lovely circling flight.

Brown leaves are flying, and soon the trees will be bare, but, to a bird artist, winter is no time of regrets for a summer past, for birds are about even in the severest weather, and sometimes a strange, rare visitor makes its appearance on the water for a time. There is no " off season " if you are interested in birds.

Tufted Duck in the Breeze

Mallard drake in eclipse plumage June 19th. No primaries visible & no inner secondaries. No curly tail feathers. Scapulars & flanks feathers brown or buff edged with sepia centres.

Head still retained small patches of glossy green feathers. Bill dull green.

Aug. 4th Much eclipse plumage still showing, but new primaries, secondaries and tail feathers well-grown Breast beginning to show a more bronze colour.

Sept. 30th Drake in complete winter plumage with no trace of eclipse plumage remaining

There is considerable variation both in the colour and the period of eclipse plumage, and it is possible to see very brown drakes with others in almost full winter plumage.

Some Plumage Studies of the Mallard Drake

Study of Shoveller Duck. Measured Drawings from a Dead Specimen

PLUMAGE STUDY

In the chapter on field work you will have noticed that the words " plumage " and " plumage changes " are frequently mentioned and will have gathered that a knowledge of changes in plumage is an indispensable part of a bird artist's equipment. So it behoves you, for a certain portion of your time, to turn yourself into an ornithologist, and, in your field work, so set down the changes you observe in the plumage of the various birds you study. *Always date your observations.* At the end of a complete year's study, you will be surprised at the number of changes recorded in your sketch book. As a further aid to understanding the changes, I suggest that you should visit a museum where you can study the skins of the birds which you have been drawing. In a good, well-kept collection each specimen is dated and sexed. More useful still would be your own exact plumage studies made from freshly killed birds. For some years, I have been in the habit of making careful measured drawings, in colour, of any dead bird which has come into my hands, providing it has been in fresh condition. Wherever possible I have drawn the birds exactly life size. I try to arrange them so that the upper surfaces, including that of the fully-opened wing, are shown : the under surfaces with

Young Wheatear. Study from life

wings in the same position : a side view with the wings closed, and any other details, such as a front view of the head, accurate studies of legs and feet, and drawings of single

Blackgame ♀.
Obtained Oct 8th
MR Schofield.
Wm Moffatt.

Tail coverts
hide the last
outer tail
feathers.

Wing 230 m.m.
Beak to Tail. 17½ inches.
A. to B. 190 m.m.
Tarse 45 m.m   Wing fully extended
about 280 m.m.

Grey Hen.   Studies from a Dead Bird

feathers,—in fact, anything which I think may be of use.   It is important that the specimen be as fresh as possible, because, apart from the unpleasant smell of a too-long dead bird, the colour of legs and bill begins to change soon after death.   Always record the colour of legs and bill from a live bird if possible.

Many of the birds I have used have been picked up in a dying condition ; in your field work you are bound to come across these unfortunates, such as an injured gull among the rocks or, in the case of small birds those which have collided with cars or telegraph wires as they were flying across a road. The main roads of Cheshire have provided me with many a study specimen. Then there is our friend the gamekeeper. As his work demands that he takes all necessary precautions to preserve his Pheasant chicks, and as the killing of Crows, Jays, Tawny Owls, Little Owls, Sparrow-hawks and Kestrels and the like is considered by him to be a part of these precautions, the

Young Cuckoo. Drawn from life

Young Herring Gull. Drawn from an Injured Bird

gamekeeper, as a potential provider of specimens, is worth remembering. In the case of a particular gamekeeper friend of mine, I have supplied him with a number of stamped, addressed postcards so that he could let me know at once of any " vermin " he may have shot.

I am fortunate, also, in knowing an expert ornithologist, who is a fine taxidermist and the keeper of a museum. Sometimes, when a fresh specimen arrived for his museum he would allow me to make my studies of the bird before he made it up into a skin for his cabinet collection.

House Sparrow. (Male)
Drawn December 3rd.

House Sparrow (Male)
Drawn October 24th.

Juvenile Male. Drawn July 20th

HOUSE SPARROW
Plumage Studies of Males

667761

DUNLIN

In the foreground is a bird in Summer Plumage; in the centre, one in Winter Plumage; the remaining two are juveniles. It is possible to see birds in all these stages of plumage at the same time.

Lapwing Chicks

To revert to the all-important study of plumage changes, let us now take one bird—say the cock Lapwing—and note the various stages of plumage through which it passes from the nestling to the adult bird, and the changes which occur in the adult during one year of its life.

Nestling.—The Lapwing chick emerges from the egg clothed with soft down and can walk almost as soon as the down is dry. Its crown, back, and wings are of a drab sepia tinge with darker sepia markings, and, when the young bird is squatting, which it does as soon as the parent gives the alarm call, this colour of crown and back bears a very close resemblance to a piece of dry dung, and the chick is most difficult to find. When it stands up, however, it has a conspicuous white collar (which was hidden in the squatting position), white under-sides, a dark bar or gorget across its chest, and grey-blue legs.

Juvenile.—By the time it is fully fledged the young Lapwing is very different in

Juvenile Lapwing

appearance. The crown is now covered with black brown-edged feathers which, at the back, terminate in a small crest ; the mantle and scapulars are of a dull metallic green edged with fawn-brown ; the wing coverts dull metallic green verging to bluish-black or greenish-black, these also edged with fawn or brown ; upper tail coverts are pale buff ; tail is half black, half white, the hinder portion being black ; each tail feather is tipped with fawn : the two outer tail feathers are all white except for a small spot of black which sometimes occurs near the tips (I have made a drawing of a specimen which had a spot on one outer tail feather but none on the other) ; sides of face buffish with a narrow dusky mark running from the corner of the gape, under the eye, to the ear coverts ; nape buffish ; chin white, the white continuing in a thin line down through the black-brown gorget which crosses the chest ; breast and flanks white ; under tail coverts pale chestnut ; legs, the front edge a warm grey, becoming a dull straw-yellow on the hinder edge ; toes a yellowish-grey.

First Winter.—In the latter part of the year the bird moults much of its first juvenile plumage and grows what is known among ornithologists as its " first winter plumage." Now we see a marked change. The young Lapwing grows a somewhat longer crest, the dark marks on the sides of the face are more definite, the dark gorget is blacker and not divided by a thin line of white, the green of mantle, scapulars, coverts and inner secondaries is rather brighter and of a more metallic quality, and certain of the scapular feathers have a purplish tinge ; the buff edges to scapulars and coverts are not so much

Lapwing in First Winter Plumage

LAPWING
Adult Male in Breeding Plumage

GREAT CRESTED GREBE
Adult Male in Breeding Plumage

edges as spots or notches of buff arranged round the tips of the feathers ; the upper tail coverts are of a buffish-chestnut and the under tail coverts, though still a pale chestnut, are brighter in colour than was the case in the juvenile plumage ; where the legs were yellowish in the juvenile they are now of a pinkish tinge.

First Summer Plumage.—The next change of plumage occurs in early spring and is known as " first summer plumage." By it our young cock Lapwing loses most of the buff edging to the scapulars, coverts, and innermost secondaries chiefly by the wearing away of the tips of the feathers, but also by a partial moulting in the early spring, so that when the breeding season arrives his upper parts are resplendent in shades of metallic green with a dash of magenta-purple on the scapulars : his head loses a good deal of its buffish tinge and takes on a greater contrast of black and white ; his chin and throat become jet black, and he is much blacker in the portion of the head between the eye and the beak. But, still scattered about his plumage are odd brown or white edges to feathers which mark him as a young bird.

Adult Male Lapwing in Winter Plumage

Head of Adult Male Lapwing.   Left—in Summer.   Right—in Winter

Second Winter Plumage.—In the fall of the year he undergoes a complete moult, and it is only when he has acquired the plumage of his second winter, that he can be said to have attained full maturity.   Now, in his second winter plumage he has a fine long crest, beautiful irridescent green back, and rich chestnut upper and under tail coverts ; and you will notice that the two new outer tail feathers, which in the juvenile were almost pure white, have acquired a pronounced black area—a narrow patch on the outer web and a broad one on the inner : notice, too, that he has lost his black throat and some of the black from his face; on his green splendour the pale buff edges appear again, but this time they are really edges and not a fringe of spots ; some of the edges, especially those on the median coverts, are almost white ; his legs are purplish-pink. Thus he will remain till the following spring, when he will again undergo that partial moult, and appear a proud bird of jet black throat and chest, shining green upper parts, rich buff-chestnut tail-coverts and legs of a brownish-pink.

I think you will agree now that a knowledge of plumage changes is important, for it would never do to put a fine cock Lapwing, in summer plumage, in the middle of a December landscape.   Remember that there is always a fierce ornithologist just round the corner, ready to pounce and rend you as soon as you make a " birdy " faux-pas.

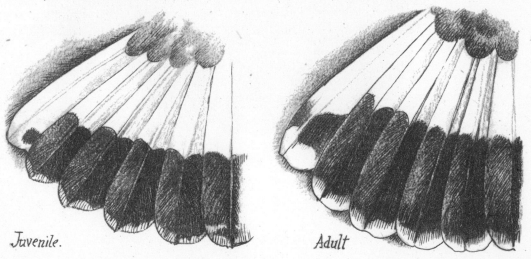

Juvenile.   *Adult*

Tails of Lapwings.   Showing the difference between the Juvenile and Adult

WOOD DUCKS

*An American species included to show the extreme
contrast between the Plumage of Duck and Drake*

BLACK-HEADED GULLS

All these stages of Plumage were observed on the same day among birds resting on the Dee weir at Chester. Reading from the top they are—Juvenile, Juvenile changing to First Winter, First Summer, Adult in Summer, Adult in Winter

Sedge Warbler.   Drawn from life while it was singing and flying about by the waterside

POSES AND ACTION STUDIES

When beginning your studies in the field you will, naturally, have given most attention to resting birds or those standing or perching, these being better models than birds that are moving. You will have noted the characteristic shape of each bird, and will have learnt much that should prove of great use to you in future picture-making. But quite as fascinating and important as the study of the resting bird is that of the bird in action.

The study of movement is difficult, but of absorbing interest. As I mentioned previously, your aim should be to get the action photographed on your mind, and then, as soon as the bird has stopped moving, or has gone out of sight, to set your impression down on paper as soon as possible, for you will discover that the longer the interval between seeing and recording, the more faded becomes the impression. As you become more practised you will find that you are able to carry a clear impression for a longer time, but it is always best to put it down on paper at once. Occasionally when I have been studying a difficult and elusive movement I have found it useful, after a period

Mallard Duck Brooding her Young. Drawn from life

PEREGRINE FALCON
Removing a flake of loose skin from its foot

GOLDEN PLOVER

Injury feigning.   Drawn from studies made in Sutherland, of a Plover which tried to entice us from the vicinity of its young. It gave us a most convincing imitation of a bird with a broken wing

at rest

at rest

at rest

Chin scratching

Wing stretching

Wing, tail and leg stretching

Turnstone poses

Turnstone.   Quick outline drawings to fix various poses

of watching, to close my eyes when beginning the drawing.   By this means I can, some-times, recall a clear vision of the bird in action, and although the resultant drawing is often disjointed, this method is good in that it eliminates all other sights which might otherwise confuse and interfere with my first fresh vision, and by it some lines of the bird are recorded truly.   It is an easy matter to assemble these disjointed but true lines in a second drawing made with the eyes open.

What can I say about the immense variety of movement of which even one bird is capable ?   For such vivacious creatures movement is the essence of life, and I have no doubt, that, as your studies progress, you will, for the purpose of picture-making, gradually prefer certain attitudes and actions above all others.   I am sure that, sooner or later, you will become engrossed in the study of the flying bird, and be filled with wonder at the beauty of its shape as it soars, glides, swoops, or speeds on its way.   And once again you will note how very individual is each kind of bird, no two specimens being quite identical in their manner of movement.   Mark well how the Coot differs from the Moorhen, the Thrush from the Blackbird, the Chaffinch from the Greenfinch and, if you will have contrast, the Wren from the Swan !

Then there are the wonderful attitudes adopted by some birds, when they are courting, in spring.   In many of these displays the birds often assume postures not seen at any other time of the year—postures which are often very beautiful, often even grotesque, but always fascinating.   Study these displays at every opportunity, for they

Tufted duck & Pochard in flock of 50 to 60

Oct 3rd.
Bosley R

Gliding down uncertain whether to alight

Flying round. No formation. Group constantly changing shape.

Plunging down

Coming head on

Alighting

Rising off the water

Pochard and Tufted Duck.   Notes made as they flew about the water

49

Buzzard. Sketch book notes made in Pembroke

Willow Warbler. Drawn immediately after watching the birds as they hunted among sallow and sycamore trees

*Common Terns. Attitudes noted when the male bird
presents a fish to the female during the breeding season*

have something strange about them, strange because one does not expect a creature like a bird to have a courtship ritual, yet ritual it is in many instances, with rules and procedures which are almost rigidly observed. Each species has its own peculiar way of expressing this spring-time emotion, and this you will readily perceive if, for instance, you compare the courting antics of the Grebe with those of the Mallard.

Fascinating too, are the poses of a bird when it is preening, for the feathers of the whole body are preened either by beak or toe, and to accomplish this the bird twists itself into all sorts of interesting attitudes. It is when studying the preening bird that you will be especially glad of your knowledge of feather groups, As the bird rummages with its beak, you will see first one set of feathers lifted, then another ; wings will be half-opened, and flight feathers will each receive careful attention, as also will the tail feathers. Preening is often accompanied by wing, tail, and leg-stretching, actions which result in novel, delectable poses for the pages of your sketch book.

For the further understanding of their action it is a good plan, sometimes, to draw, in sequence, a bird's movements as they actually occur : for instance, in watching a Kestrel hunting you would naturally begin with a sketch of the hovering position ;

Oyster-catcher. Some preening poses

Budgerigar poses

then a quick note of its appearance as it slips out of the hover to descend a little lower ; then another hovering note, which may not be quite the same as the first because the bird may be hovering in a different current of air ; then the quick descent on to its prey ; and, last of all, its action as it beats up from its find.   You may see it rise with a mouse dangling from one foot, or even a young rabbit.   When you have recorded such a sequence of movements you will feel that you know a little more about the appearance of the bird.

Kestrel hunting. Hovering in a fairly strong breeze which the. blowing up the sand dunes, this upward current accounting for the nearly horizontal hovering position

Hovering

Slipping out of the hover

Hovering at a lower level

Flying off with prey dangling from one foot.

Dropping onto its prey.

Kestrel.   A sequence of notes made when the bird was hunting

COLOUR AND TONE

If we were asked to describe the colour of a Swan or a Blackbird, most of us, I think, would answer " white " and " black " respectively. Admittedly, this plain description is sufficient for identification purposes, but it is woefully inadequate to describe the true colour of either bird for our purpose of picture-making. You will very soon realise that black is not the colour of the Blackbird, especially if the sun is shining on him, and though he is perched among green leaves he is still not black ; even in grey winter his blackness is of a different quality from that of the dark silhouettes of the bare branches which surround him.

Let us consider what is usually described as the " white " plumage of a fully adult Mute Swan, and the changes it undergoes under varying conditions of light and surroundings. It will not require a great effort on your part to perceive that, in a good light, his plumage is anything but white. Notice the yellow tinge in the feathers of neck and upper breast, and the cold bluish purity of the back, wings and tail. Note also the colour of the shadowed under-surfaces, and how it is influenced by the colour of the ground on which

Swan.   In bright sunlight against a background of dark reflections

Swan.   Silhouetted against the bright water

the bird is standing : if he is standing on green grass, then the under-parts reflect a greenish colour, whereas if he were on dry, golden sand, the reflected colour would be of a distinctly warm tint ; or, again, if he were flying over water his breast, belly and under-wings would take on a colder tint, especially if the water were reflecting a blue or grey sky.

Let us blow away the clouds and allow the sun to shine on our Swan now swimming majestically past the mere-side wood. What a transformation takes place ! The bright light turns his back to a dazzling whiteness in which there is a tinge of gold or yellow : the shadows on his plumage are now blue to violet until they reach the under-sides on which you will see much reflected light from the water. Look especially at the colour of the shadows cast by the feathers of the raised plumes of the wings ; you will see that the sun is able to penetrate through the vanes of the plumes and, in their depths, the shadows are of a different hue from those on the body of the Swan, being greenish—even golden-green. . . . . . . Our Swan is moving out from the reflection of the dark trees, against which he looks very dazzling, into the bright sky-reflecting water. Soon he swims into a position in which both he and the sun are directly in front. In this view only his upper surfaces are lit by the sunlight, the rest of him being in shadow and appearing dark violet against the bright water ; in fact, but for the light on his back and the top of his head he appears as a dark silhouette in relation to the high tone of the water . . . . . .He is going to fly ! Except for the flash of white on his neck, wings, and tail he still looks a dark bird as he thrashes and thuds his way over the water to gain impetus for flight. Now he is airborne, as the airmen say, and, as he rises in front

Flying Swan.   Looking dark against a light sky

of a dark bank of trees, he looks a very white bird, but the moment he is above the trees and has the sky for a background he again becomes a dark shape with only his upper parts catching the light.   Had the sky been full of cloud or even of a deep summer blue, and had the sun been at our backs while we were watching the flying Swan, he would have looked lighter in tone than the sky.   Suppose we visit the Swan again in mid-winter, after there has been a fall of snow, and we find him standing on the snow-covered ice of the mere.   Yes, that is our same " white " Swan, but will you, ever again, say that he is a white bird ?   Now you see how yellow his neck is and, to a lesser extent, the rest of his upper plumage.   Note also the reflected snow-light on his under-sides, which makes them look almost the same tone as, or even lighter than, his top surfaces. If he would only fly, the wonderful effect of this reflected light on his under-wings would be a revelation to you.   But no part of him can match the dazzling whiteness of the snowy expanse which surrounds him, indeed, he looks almost drab compared with it. So much for the " snow-white " Swan !

Here, then, are but a few of the infinite number and variety of conditions under which you will see birds if you continue with your studies from the life.   Few as they are they will serve to show you that a bird, in reality, has no local colour, but is always influenced by the colour and light of its surroundings.   To note and depict some of these is a labour for yourself alone.

Swan resting on snow-covered ice

Rooks in the light of a Winter Afternoon Sun. Note that the tone of their sunlit Plumage is lighter than that of the cloudy sky

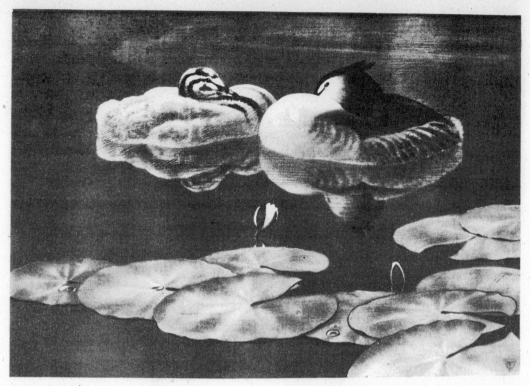

Grebe and Young in a setting of Still Water and Lily Leaves

SETTINGS

When you begin to make pictures from your bird-studies you will immediately encounter the problem of composing them in suitable settings and against appropriate backgrounds ; and, perhaps, when you remember to have seen a particularly exciting group of birds in a fine setting you will, as I have often done, bemoan the fact that you did not make as close a study of the surrounding habitat as you did of the birds themselves. For it is in this matter of settings that so many bird pictures fail. Often the bird is painted skilfully, but its surroundings " fizzle out " into a doubtful and uncertain hotch-potch of unstudied details which ruin the picture.

If you would see fine examples of bird-painting in which the settings have been given the same meticulous care as the birds themselves, you have but to study the work of the Chinese painters. Note the exquisite drawing of flower and branch, tussock, reed, and bamboo, an exquisiteness which does not detract one jot from the importance of the bird, but which does give a precious and lovely quality to the work. You might also spare some time to look at the work of John James Audubon, who did such admirable work in drawing and painting the birds of America. His attitude towards birds was not purely an artistic one, as he was a fine ornithologist for his time. His work was scientific in intention. Nevertheless, it was also artistically excellent, a combination of qualities which is woefully lacking in many modern text-books on birds. He, too, was particularly careful in drawing habitat, and among his plates there are some beautiful renderings of flowers, branches, leaves and bark.

You will see, therefore, that it would be wise to collect much information about all sorts of things to be used as settings, and you cannot begin too soon on this very necessary branch of study. While you are thus engaged do not forget to draw nests and eggs ; often, particularly in the case of sea-birds and waders, they are placed in most beautiful surroundings. As you will have found that there are birds to be studied all the year through, so you will realise that the study of their environments is an all-the-year occupation also, for each season brings its own wealth, variety, and change of material to be drawn, these changes being as important to note as the seasonal changes in the plumages of the birds themselves. New grass and the opening bud will accompany a particular plumage in your bird, the full bloom another, and the fringe of ice and hoar-frost on the grasses yet another. Besides these changes, there are habitats which are not influenced by, and are not indicative of any one season : for instance, the formation of sand by the sea's edge, and the wave and ripple of water. Water is a lifetime's study in itself : a most elusive substance, endless in its forms and effects, and difficult to draw and paint. The simplest seeming ripple is a most complex thing, for it has no colour of its own but reflects that of its surroundings. When you consider how many reflecting

Nest and Eggs of a Ring Plover on a Shingle Beach in Anglesey

surfaces there are on a small ripple, its complexity will no longer surprise you.   Study reflections carefully for they are always beautiful.   Those in still water are perhaps the most beautiful of all, for there you have a repetition of shape which can be most decorative. You will, however, note that it is not quite an exact duplication of the form which is reflected.   If a bird is standing in still water which is below your eye level its reflection will show more of the underside and less of the upper surfaces than is seen in the actual bird.   Should the model move slightly, and send out even the tiniest ripple, how complicated do the reflections instantly become !   The sharply outlined image is sharp

Study of a Thaw.   Dark patches of grass showing through the snow,
and the ice melting near the bank

Ring Plover and Redshank in a setting of Seaweed-covered Rock and Sand Pools. The ebbing tide leaves an endless variety of beautiful patterns on sandy beaches

Study of Stones, Water and Butterbur.   Drawn by the River Dane

no longer but is rocked and distorted by the convex and concave surfaces of the ripple . . . . Frost, snow and ice, in their endless variety of pattern and shape, are worthy of the closest attention.

In some of your bird pictures, particularly those of flying birds, you will at times want to depict a wide expanse of lansdcape and sky ; so, among many other things, here is yet another line of study to tackle, for bird-painting obviously demands that you should be something of a landscape painter.   Your days will be very full.

RED GROUSE

Two Hens and a Cock in a setting of Moorland and Hilly Landscape. (The size of the coping stones in the foreground gives the correct scale to the birds)

PICTURE MAKING

We will now assume that you have accumulated a good many drawings from life, and have made some plumage studies, and are still anxious to begin picture-making with your material. What an enormous field of expression is now open to you ! There are so many ways of making pictures with birds, and so many uses for these pictures that it would be a mistake to say, " It should be done this way or that way." You will develop your own style according to your nature and inclination. But there are certain decisions about your work which you will have to make before you start, especially with regard to treatment. Shall it be naturalistic or decorative ? It may be that in your field studies you have been very interested in the effect of light and shade on the plumage, and the atmosphere which surrounds the bird and its habitation : this being so, you will probably choose to do a naturalistic rendering of your subject. On the

Black-backed Gulls.   A naturalistic rendering

other hand, you may have been struck by the decorative qualities of birds and plants, and will therefore think of your picture in terms of decorative effect, and will be more concerned with line and pattern, and not so much with light and shade and atmosphere. Whatever your approach, you will find that your naturalistic treatment can have a very decorative quality, and that a decorative treatment can create an illusion of atmosphere though none has been consciously attempted.

Sooner or later, after you have made experiments for yourself, I think you will come to the conclusion that, however you approach the subject of bird-painting, a certain delicacy and incisiveness of treatment is called for by the very nature of your subject matter. In my opinion, a heavy technique does not suit our subject. My best results have been obtained from the use of the graver on wood, from the delicacy of water-colour and tempera, and from a particular technique of oil-painting in which the use of thin

Pheasant in the Rain. A decorative treatment

WIDGEON

BARNACLE GEESE

Goldcrest on a Larch branch

paint allowed the texture of the unprimed material to play a big part in the appearance of the finished painting.

In spite of this call for delicate handling, prettiness, I think, should be avoided at all costs. Birds are too alive and vital to be merely pretty, many are grand and dignified, but even the tiny Goldcrest has a quick incisiveness about it that saves it from mere prettiness. When we consider birds as big as Geese, what strength and grandeur of line and form we have!

Careful attention should be given to composition and scale; by scale I allude to the relation of the bird to its surroundings. It would be quite justifiable to paint a spacious landscape as a background to a skein of Geese, for a formation of flying Geese, at a distance of fifty yards, can span quite a large portion of landscape. But it would hardly be correct to use that same landscape behind a company of Blue Tits on a twig; for how much landscape would these tiny mites require? A few leaves and a little patch of sky would suffice for them. The amateur almost always blunders in this matter of scale, and often, by attempting too much background, causes his Kingfishers to appear as big as Eagles, and his Pied Wagtails the size of Geese.

In the matter of treatment I always try to do the finished work quickly and without labouring the technique. This mode of procedure often requires much preparation in the shape of rough sketches and preliminary trials. It requires that all details should be absolutely settled before the finished work is commenced. For such work as wood-engraving it is imperative that you should be quite certain of your intentions before you begin, for once a cut is made on the block it cannot be erased. Water-colour work should also be preceded by rough sketches and colour schemes, so that the finished work may be

White Chinese Geese

carried out without hesitation and fumbling ; for, among the various media, water-colour especially gains by a quick, direct application of pigment to paper. My oil paintings are also the result of much previous planning and are, as a rule, executed direct in one application of the paint.

However, you may find that a delicate technique does not suit you and that you prefer slashing brush strokes of thick oil paint with which to express yourself. That is a matter for you to decide : there are no hard and fast rules and regulations concerning self expression in paint or any other medium. Remember, too, that your bird portrait is not complete until you have satisfactorily settled the vital matter of presentation. The correct frame for your oil-painting, the exact mount and frame for your water-colour, or the nice matching of your engraved book illustration with its surrounding type are matters of the greatest importance, and should have as much thought and care lavished upon them as has been given to the picture itself. The frame either separates it from or connects it with its environments but always affects the quality of the picture which it surrounds ; it is the actual completion of your work.

GREY WAGTAIL—Autumn

WOOD WARBLER—Spring

Red-throated Divers on a Sutherland Loch

A DAY OF DAYS

As you proceed with your picture-making I think you will realise the value of all the field work you have done, and how essential it is to the maintaining of freshness in your work, a freshness which is as the breath of life to your creations. Therefore, you will keep up your drawing from live birds, and continually increase your knowledge of, and pleasure in them. Birds are so variable in their behaviour that there is no danger of exhausting their possibilities, and the study of them will take you into wild and beautiful places, one or two of which will stand out clear in your memory above all others. This has been my experience, and the following is an account of one perfect day which I have a great longing to repeat whenever I recall it.

The time was June and the place was Sutherland. My wife and I had made our centre at a house on Badcall Bay, and had spent a wonderful fortnight among the hills, lochs and lochans, and the shores of this wild corner of Sutherland, chiefly to study the Red-throated Diver. I had succeeded in finding and drawing several pairs of these interesting birds, until they had become as familiar as old friends. We had heard and read many accounts of the bird-life on Handa Island, and all the time we were working on the Divers there was, at the back of our minds, a fixed intention to visit the place, for we could see one corner of it from the Badcall cliffs. It lay some miles to the North, and only a narrow Sound separated it from the mainland, but so far either the sea had been too rough for a landing, or the weather had not been suitable for bird drawing.

However, one day during the first week in June, near the end of our stay, the sun shone brilliantly, the sea was calm, and we decided early that it was a " Handa " day. We made our way by the winding roads curving round beautiful lochs and between rocky hills, lilac-pink in colour, until we arrived at a place where the road dropped steeply down to the sea. Not far from the sea we came to Tarbet—a mere cluster of white cottages built on the wild hillside, where between the rocky outcrops tiny fields of potatoes were tilled. We knocked at the door of one of the cottages, and our knock was answered by an aged woman whose wrinkled weather-beaten face told of much work in the fields. When we enquired about the possibility of crossing to Handa she called her son, a big man with a limp, and he accompanied us to the foot of the hill. This ended suddenly at a shingle beach where boats were pulled up beyond the high-tide marks. Soon we were in one of the boats, and were being rowed steadily across the half-mile-wide Sound of Handa.

Handa Sound from Tarbet Beach

RED-THROATED DIVERS

EIDER DUCK

Eider Duck and Drake and Black Guillemots

The water was so clear that the sun lit up the gently waving forests of seaweed to a great depth. Birds were all around us, and some allowed the boat to approach close before troubling either to dive or fly. Fat, contented-looking Eider Ducks rested on the edges of the little islets of the Sound; others floated near our boat or flew close above our heads. That very neat little bird, the Black Guillemot, also kept us company. Our boatman told us that these birds nest on one particular island in the Sound, and nowhere else in the vicinity. Their striking white wing patches and bright red legs flashed and glowed as the " Tysties " flew by in the bright, clear light. (Tystie is another name for the Black Guillemot). Common Guillemots swam about the Sound, and these were much shyer than their black cousins, for they dived long before the boat was upon them. Razorbills swam with heads held high and tails pointing skywards, and they, too, were shy.

Common Guillemots, Razorbills and Black Guillemots

We first set foot on Handa in a tiny rock-bound bay which was sheltered from the main current of the Sound by rocky islets. Having arranged with our boatman to meet him at the landing place at six in the evening, we shouldered our tackle, and made our way across the island. The weather was hot, and before we had proceeded far we wished we had left raincoats and the like at home. We climbed and toiled, our path ever rising over rock and rough grass, past a derelict farmhouse and a flock of startled Cheviot sheep, until we came eventually to the highest point of the island, from which we could look down to the edges of the high cliffs facing the open sea. And now we were given a hint of what we should see on the cliffs themselves, for, weaving about in the air above them, were many birds, chiefly Herring Gulls and Fulmar Petrels. The sight of the Fulmars lent wings to our feet, and we hurried from the high ground down to the cliff edge. What a sight then met our gaze ! The air below us was alive with flying birds—Fulmars, Guillemots, Razorbills, Kittiwakes, and Herring and Black-backed Gulls. But their numbers were as nothing to the multitudes which crowded the ledges and crannies of the cliff face. We gazed in amazement at the spectacle of so much bird life : the upper ledges of the cliffs were occupied by the nestling Fulmars and a few Razorbills, then came rank upon rank of Razorbills, and below these were thousands of Guillemots ; lowest of all nested the Kittiwakes. The noise, and the

The Edge of the Cliff

RAZORBILLS

smell, was prodigious. By the base of the cliffs, and for a good distance out, swam rafts of Guillemots and Razorbills, and there was a continuous traffic of birds between the water and the cliff face. Close by us the Fulmars glided about the cliff top on set, rigid wings, soaring, banking, descending, and soaring again with never a wing-beat as they used the ascending currents of air about the cliff. Those lovely, gentle Fulmars! We could have watched them for hours as they glided past, sometimes not more than five yards from us. Other Fulmars were just below us, on the nestling ledges, and were not alarmed at our presence. They made perfect models, their only movement being

The Cliffs of Handa

Fulmar Sketches

Fulmars Billing and Cooing

a gentle, slow swaying of their heads as they regarded us. I set to work with pencil and sketch book and made as many studies as I desired, mostly without the aid of field glasses, so close were they. I seized this opportunity to make really exhaustive notes of the colour of beak, legs and feet. The only cause of disturbance to my best Fulmar model was the arrival of its mate beside it. This was a most interesting and rather touching performance. Sometimes the mate had to make several attempts before it could effect a landing beside the sitting bird, for the Fulmar's legs and feet are not very strong, and only occasionally does it stand on its webbed toes. Normally it rests on the full foot. When it finally came to rest, what a billing and cooing began ! The sitting bird nuzzled its bill into the breast feathers of its mate, which bent its head in, what seemed to me, an ecstacy of avian affection. Then both birds began to talk, " quock ! quock ! quock !," throats distended, necks swaying, heads now held high, now bent low to the rock. The talk became quicker and quicker, and was suddenly brought to a close when the lately arrived mate stood for a moment on its toes, and took off from the ledge in a graceful, descending swoop. Later, a dapper Razorbill landed close by and was greeted by a vicious hiss from the sitting Fulmar. The Razorbill then made a hasty nose-dive from the ledge. Some of the Fulmars were nesting on ledges covered by the pink flowers and green cushions of the sea-pink, which made an exquisite setting for the creamy-white and silvery-grey plumage of the birds.

We walked slowly along the cliff top, gazing our fill at the birds, all the time accompanied by the bedlam of cries made by the Kittiwakes and Guillemots below. At times we peered over the edge to the dizzy depths four hundred feet below, to where

Cormorants and Shags

the Cormorants and the Shags rested on the flat tables of rock at sea-level, their dark erect shapes contrasting sharply with the white foam of the swell breaking below them. On one sunlit rock a Greater Black-backed Gull was absorbed in devouring a Kittiwake. The Black-back jabbed and thrust with blood-stained beak at the breast of the little Gull, and was soon devouring its entrails. The delicate white feathers which had been torn away floated gently about the flat rock—there was scarce breeze enough to move them.

A little further on we were brought to a standstill by the sight of a Puffin perched on a jutting-out shoulder of cliff some fifteen feet below us. When we drew near it flew off, but soon returned to its perch again. Several times it did this, always returning to the same place and, strangely enough, taking up the same position each time. So out came the sketch book and I made a useful study of its three-quarters back view, which it always presented to me. Here again I carefully noted down the colour of the amazing beak, legs, eyes, and the peculiar tab of skin above and below the eyes. A most obliging bird was this, for we did not see many Puffins, and those we did see had their nesting burrows in a steep, grass-covered slope of a fallen cliff several hundred feet down.

Our next move brought us to the most spectacular part of the island, where the cliffs are probably at their highest. Here, separated from the cliffs by only a narrow channel of water, is a huge stack of rock whose summit is level with the top of the cliff.

Puffin.   A most obliging bird

This stack must once have been part of the cliff itself, but centuries of wild Atlantic gales have isolated it.   On it, thousands upon thousands of birds were nesting or resting. The flat top of the stack was covered by a tumultuous host of Guillemots which yelled and squabbled continually.   When two birds decided to fight they just staggered over the top of their neighbours, regardless of the protesting cries and pecks from those they trampled upon.   There was no bare rock on which to fight on the top of that congested stack !   Lower down the sides of the stack many Kittiwakes were nesting.   They were as noisy as the Guillemots, and a never-ending chorus of " Gitty werk ! Gitty werk !" came from them.   The brooding Kittiwakes sat on their whitened nest piles (which seemed to cling to the rock only by some miraculous means) with their heads towards the rock face, and their tails directed outwards.   Each time they were visited by their

Kittiwake Sketches

mates they yelled at the top of their voices, and the sound of the massed chorus was echoed back from the precipitous cliffs—a thrilling noise. We had been so engrossed by the amazing sight of the stack and its population that we had failed to notice a small group of three Guillemots squatting in a pocket of rock not more than fifteen feet away from us. They were in the full glare of the sun and seemed to enjoy their siesta in that hot, smelly hollow, and were so quiet that I started to draw them at once. They sat and peered at me with much neck-stretching, and appeared to commune with one another as to the best course to pursue. Finally, they remained and were quiet again, except when I made a slight movement which gave rise to more questioning neck-stretching. Lovely to be able to draw wild birds without having to use field glasses ! I made a detailed drawing of them, and then we moved on. How quickly the time was passing !

Soon we came to a place where there was a huge hole in the cliffs, an enormous black funnel at the bottom of which the sea surged and foamed through a narrow arch. No birds nested on the black walls of this dreadful place, nor was it good for humans to look down into it for too long a time. We were glad to avert our gaze and to regard the lovely drifts of sea-pinks which here covered the cliff tops and the upper ledges. Here again Fulmars and Razorbills and also Herring Gulls were nesting, and some of the resulting colour schemes made by the birds, flowers and rocks were inexpressibly beautiful. I made several notes, before we continued on our way round the cliffs. Presently, in a depression of the headland, we came upon a little blue lochan, and by its shore stood a solitary Oyster-catcher. It had a white ring round its neck, greyish

Guillemot siesta

legs, and a bill which was a dull yellow with a dark tip, details which denoted a year old bird.   Adults at this time of the year have no white ring, their bills are bright orange and vermilion, and their legs are a rosy-pink.

On again : and now the height of the cliffs gradually diminished until we found ourselves but a few feet above sea-level, and on the edge of shelving rocks.   Here we decided to have tea and feast upon the beauty of land and sea, as well as upon sandwiches. We had now nearly circled the island, and were once more facing the Sutherland main-land, and were looking towards the south where the hazy blue silhouettes of Quinag, Canisp, and Suilven filled the far horizon with their grand shapes, and the Bay of Edrachillis glittered in the sunlight.   On a flat-topped rock a hundred feet away, Shags and Cormorants rested in a dark group, some of them with wings wide open to the sun. Judging by the whiteness of that rock it must have been a favourite resting place.   A furtive movement by the edge of the brown seaweed below attracted our attention, and soon the movement became a brown shape—that of an Eider Duck with a brood of ducklings close-packed at her tail.   Hurriedly she took them away from our vicinity,

Where we had Tea

Eider Duck and her Brood

hugging rocks and seaweed closely, her brood always swimming at her tail in a solid group. They were soon hidden from our gaze by a jutting rock.

While eating our sandwiches we had casually noted a pair of Oyster-catchers which hung about the rocks. They seemed to be most uneasy at our presence, and when we got to our feet, their agitation increased, and soon they were flying round us in circles, calling shrilly. We began to examine the ground. Suddenly Winifred pointed to a tiny shape which was running swiftly away. I gave chase and succeeded in putting my hat over it. I then felt underneath, and pulled out a fluffy Oyster-catcher chick. The parents were now in a perfect frenzy of alarm, but I was determined to get some information about that chick in spite of their heart-rending calls. I placed it in Winifred's hand and it remained quiet while I drew. Having completed a drawing of its upper

Oyster-catcher Chick.   Upper surface

Oyster-catcher Chick.   Under-side

surface I now wanted to draw its under-sides, so turned it over on to its back, in which position it lay as quiet as before until I had completed that view also.   Then it was

No more posing !

Hooded Crows and their Egg Larder

placed on the ground, and immediately ran away, as fast as it could go, over the rough grass and up into the rocky outcrops above the shore, escorted by its distracted parents.

A glance at my watch revealed that we had only a little time left before six o'clock, so reluctantly we left our beautiful shore and struck inland in the direction of our landing place. We came to a tiny stream which ran down a peaty gully. From it a pair of Hooded Crows hurriedly flew up, and on reaching the spot where they had been we saw scores of egg-shells, mostly of Guillemots and Razorbills, with a few Herring Gull and Kittiwake shells also. All were in the gully by the stream side. We examined them and brought away some of the more beautifully marked fragments, the two Hoodies watching us all the time from a rocky hillock near by. We were amused to find among the egg-shells a ping-pong ball, which had been neatly punctured and must have been a source of great disappointment and disgust to the Hoodies. Another collection of shell fragments was found in a second gully. The Crows must have had very

Towards Tarbet and the Mainland

successful hunting among the cliff birds, and it was interesting to speculate on how and why the eggs had all found their way to the gullies. Scrambling over rocks, rough pasture, and a stream where yellow irises were blooming, we eventually came in sight of the little rocky bay on Handa Sound. We were a little disappointed to find our boatman waiting for us, for any excuse to linger on Handa this day would have been a good one.

The waters of the Sound had a smooth glassiness which was only slightly disturbed by the rising tide. The early evening sunlit cliffs and islets with a golden glow, and turned the breasts of the Eider Drakes a wonderful rosy-yellow. The scarlet feet of the Tysties looked vermilion in this light.

The same birds, Eiders, Guillemots, and Razorbills, kept us company across the Sound, and all too soon we arrived at the rocky jetty at Tarbet, where the high tide was gently lapping the lowest of a pile of lobster-pots. White hens were scratching about in the dried seaweed near the beached boats. We climbed the steep road past the little white cottages, paid our boatman, and made our way back to Scourie. The great rocky piles of Fionaven and Arkle loomed above the shoulders of the near hills, and the lochs reflected the colour of bronze-green heather and rose-pink rock perfectly, for there was scarcely a breeze. As we passed by a stream, a pair of Mergansers skittered up from a pool and flew off down stream towards the sea. Slowly we made for Badcall, while Cuckoos called from the rowan trees on the islets in the lochs, and Sandpipers flew up from their shores. When we reached the house at Badcall, we saw in the quiet waters of the Bay a pair of Mergansers, an immature Red-throated Diver, and, on one of the little islands, a small group of Arctic Terns, besides the usual Eiders resting at the edge of the water. That night a Cuckoo was heard calling at midnight, for it never became really dark at any time, and very early next morning we awoke to the calls of the Arctic Terns which skimmed and flickered above the quiet water of the bay.

Red-breasted Mergansers, Eiders and Arctic Terns

House Sparrows

IN CONCLUSION

I think you will agree that the day I have described in the previous pages was one to gladden the heart of anyone interested in birds. I admit that we saw no rarities, but we did not set out to look for them. We were in quest of material for picture-making, and as, for this purpose, any bird is a good model, we found riches indeed. It is exciting to see a rarity, but only because it is a rarity : its artistic possibilities are not necessarily superior to those of a commoner bird. As a subject the Great Crested Grebe is as good as the Slavonian Grebe (perhaps better), the Lapwing as good as the Hoopoe, and the Kestrel as the rarest of the Harriers. It is clear then, that all the materials for bird pictures lies quite close at hand, and your chief concern will be to find that particular method of presentation which best suits you and your subject. Problems of line, composition, design, and colour, all must be studied thoroughly ; for your bird pictures, like all other pictures, will not be successful unless these matters are dealt with completely and effectively. There is a rich field of reference open to you : if you lean towards the precious, exquisite treatment, you will find no better masters than the early Chinese bird painters ; or if towards the careful, detailed rendering, our good friend Audubon will no doubt inspire you ; or again, if towards an acutely naturalistic treatment, the work of Bruno Liljefors, the Scandinavian artist, is better than most.

But the greatest teacher of them all will be the living bird amid the air, light, foliage, grass or water which surrounds it. Only by the study of birds themselves can you hope to develop an individual style. And, though you may never be satisfied with your own work, you will derive much pleasure from this study, and from your growing acquaintance with these strange, beautiful creatures, and in time you may impart some of that pleasure to those who see your efforts at Bird Portraiture.

Song Thrush

Little Owl